In the name of God, the Most Merciful, the Merciful

Glory be to God

God is free from imperfection and all praise is due to Him

God is free from imperfection, The Greatest

There is no power and no strength except with God

I seek forgiveness from God.

Prose of The Travelling Soul

Short Accounts of My Journey To Islam

Amina G

Michael Terence Publishing

First published in paperback by
Michael Terence Publishing in 2020
www.mtp.agency

Copyright © 2020 Amina G

Amina G has asserted the right to be identified as the
author of this work in accordance with the
Copyright, Designs and Patents Act 1988

ISBN 9781800940987

No part of this publication may be reproduced, stored in a retrieval system, or transmitted, in any form or by any means, electronic, mechanical, photocopying, recording or otherwise, without the prior permission of the publishers

Cover images
Copyright © Jianye Li
www.123rf.com

Cover design
Copyright © 2020 Michael Terence Publishing

I did not change my life to hurt you, I changed it to save me.

Travelling soul

My home is not in this world
My heart belongs not to this world but my Creator.
I am a travelling soul,
Journeying in this life,
Until I'm home.

Everyone has a story. We are living our stories. In this world as it is, not everybody gets to live their story on the lands in which they were born. For others, their stories don't end on the lands where they flourished.

Affection for this life has consequences. One should grasp the virtues of being content with who they are by living in the present, being in the moment. The virtues of gratitude, prayer and removing all attachment to the material possessions of this world. This is the food of life to give nourish to the heart and soul.
The existence of God is real,
though we are not willing to believe it.

Amina G

For me, my story began some place in the lands of Africa. The cultures, the people, and all of the colours of Africa continue to live within my soul. Somewhere deep inside, in silence, I still breathe the tales of Africa.

This is the short account of my story. In reflections and poetry, it tells my journey from Africa, to the west, to embracing Islam.

Castles in the air

Growing up, I was meant to be seen and not heard.

My needs were burdens

My pleas for love were nauseating

My cries were an annoyance

My pain, frivolous.

Still, I pestered for love and care

I felt I deserved.

Strange is the tenacity of a child.

The cries and tantrums that shout

Demanding clear and loud,

"You will love me, I won't stop until you love me."

I fought hard for the love of my stepmother.

I roared, she thundered.

Amina G

I punched, she bruised.
I stood tall, she kicked me to the ground.

Again and again, we continued
Until my bruises turned to wounds.
The wounds emptying my pains
My child frame couldn't swallow.

Whereupon in despair and desolation
I developed a love for daydreaming.
One by one,
I would build each castle in the air.

Building Castles again... *Chizero*

Building castles in the air,
A threatening doing.
Unbeknownst is the destruction,
when they crush to the ground.

It had become something of a habit. The pleasant destructive thoughts, to escape the truth of my existence. Emotional, mental and physical violation at the hands of my stepmother, Amai. Everything about me as she saw it, had been something of a theatre piece. How do you perceive someone who does not so much as try to pronounce your name correctly?

Giselle. "Chizero," she called me. In Shona, it means it's a zero, a loser. Every day, several times a day, I was Chizero, a loser. On top of the beatings, the insults and degradation meant that when I saw a reflection of myself, I did not see anything but a loser.

Yes... building castles in the air was the perfect escapism, until the unfortunate day when a terrible traumatic memory hindered. Suddenly, it seemed my life had been "okay" after all.

Chizero.

Before, the castles came tumbling down.
The beatings. The insults. The humiliation and,
the shame that came with it.
It was discipline, she had said,
To give direction.
It had been "okay"... Undamaged... Unbroken.

The mental hurts. The physical hurts.
My heart in flames.
It had been "okay"... Undamaged... Unbroken.
Before, the castles came tumbling down.

The flashback

How could it be that it had disappeared from my memory all of that time, to return during the saddest moment when I felt unloved, unwanted and completely alone.

By the time I was eleven, I had mastered the art of daydreaming to the point where I could be in a house full of people, noise, chit-chat and laughter and, I would not hear a single word. I would escape to a different experience which was not mine. A bubble where I was loved and wanted. I felt like I was part of something extraordinary in this place. I often escaped to this world to remove the sadness I felt and emotions of the kind that I could not discern.

But this vision that I was seeing was bona fide. It was undeniable and it was not something my eleven years old self could dream up. The images were vivid and the hurt felt real. The surroundings were familiar. I saw a flash of his face… then pain… and the soiled bed.

Panic-stricken, I opened my eyes, but the fear had caused me to fall off my bed as I tried now to escape from my existent nightmare.

I realise now, that this was the first time my life crushed, and my childhood ended.

#metoo #ithappenedtome

Flashes of the past,

albeit passed.

The genesis of my ruin.

Playing with my friends.

Happy-go-lucky, not a care for the world.

Ignorant from its laments.

My childhood stolen by the impiety of some other.

I must have been a little younger than five,

the end of my life, as I had known it.

Now,

as the flashes of my past return,

this interruption has suddenly become a daily grind

To stay alive.

Changed

I cannot describe how it felt to have self-contempt and blame amplify. It was before then, alive and cooking inside of me. I can tell you though that on most days, I couldn't breathe. I was now often in a state of inner turmoil and had begun to hate leaving the house, even if it was to buy a loaf of bread, which was something Amai would often instruct me to do. I hated it, but I did it. It was an unforgivable act to refuse to follow directions or refuse to do daily chores and, a lot involved leaving the house in order to get things done. I often had to do these on my own. Going out to the shops had now become most frightening. The sound of a man walking behind me, or the sight of him walking ahead of me or towards me, would put me in a state of extreme fear and unease that I struggled to breathe.

A man was walking towards me and going past me once, I don't remember anything else except seeing his white teeth and his shoulders bobbing up and down. After he left and was out of sight, I realised that he had been laughing. My behaviour might have been unusual to him. It was as if he deemed me mad and abnormal. This had become my reality. Everything about me, how I perceived myself and inside my head had modified. I did not investigate any further about the flashback. I knew it happened and it was true. It appeared in my dreams. It made me hate, blame myself, wallow in self-pity and sadness. More so, I felt lonelier. That was enough. I wanted to rip my soul out and give it to death. This body of mine was done. The moment it took birth in my daydream, in that burst, I was changed.

How did I get here?

My life deflected.

Yesterday, I was Chizero.

Nothing but a loser.

Today, still Chizero, I am poorer. Wretched.

My burdens loaded.

Terror fills my core.

Amina G

Fear keeps me agitated.
Perturbation, my life's sore.
Feels like my head is contaminated.
Mentally deranged.

I am changed.

The affairs of my sleeps

Such is the mind's eye

One cannot fathom.

I am at rock bottom.

In the restless nights.

Glimpse images of anamnesis sparse,

Enough to engender conflicting feelings.

I can hear my heart racing.

Struggling for breath,

My body feels numb

My heart weeping.

Sweating

Shaking

My body is helpless.

Still, I fight to breathe again.

With my head turning violently from left to right.

My body still shaking,

I fight.

I fight to wake up.

WAKE UP.

These were the affairs of my sleeps for almost 18 years after the flashback.

Conscious,

Still shaking,

I prompt myself to breathe.

All is well.

Simply breathe,

For now...

The phone call

A little while after the flashback, I was at a family wedding. Preferring my own company, I scrambled past a table stacked with snacks, picked up a packet of 'Thingz' (a salty snack which is similar to Wotsits) and walked out of the hall. I was standing by a tree that was near a car park and admiring the cars at rest whilst oblivious to my surroundings. Suddenly, a hand appeared in my packet of 'Thingz' and then disappeared. I looked to my side to search for the owner of the hand. It was him. It was my cousin from the flashback. In shock, I dropped my packet on the floor and stared. I stopped breathing, and yet I could hear the sound of my heart beating loud. I'm not sure if he noticed my shock because he spoke as if he had been a part of my life all the while. All of the five or six years of it since I had last seen him. I think he said something about delicious 'Thingz' and other things I did not hear, and then he walked away, as if nothing had ever happened. As if he had never done anything bad. I must have stood by that tree for a while before I went back into the hall. I don't remember seeing him or how I got home that day.

I cannot recall the length of time after the wedding, but somehow his appearance in our household had now become a regularity. I made it a priority to avoid him. If he ever spoke to me, I couldn't respond or, I didn't respond. When he was there, I would go to the house next door where my friend lived. I felt shocked and surprised at how he made everything seem normal. He acted as we were and had been best friends forever. When he didn't visit, he would regularly telephone us at our house.

On one occasion, he called whilst I was at home alone. I picked up the phone not expecting him to be on the other end. As soon as I heard his voice, I felt a rage inside that I had never experienced before. I suddenly realised, I hated him. He was talking but I was not listening. The sound of his voice became so extremely exasperating, that I cursed under my breath and hung up on him as he was still talking. Screaming, I beat the phone on its holder a few times before throwing it to the other end of the room. It hit the wall and fell onto the carpeted floor. My only fortune, the phone didn't break otherwise I would have had to explain myself to Amai. Alone in the house but not wanting to be dramatic, I fell to my knees and began to cry. I never heard from him or saw him again after that.

The vow

On top of Amai's perpetual violation, I was sent to a boarding school where, in my opinion, the education system obliterated your poise. The teachers damned you for the hurt or pain afflicted upon you and kicked you while you were down. They would beat you senseless because you misspelt a word in an essay or you got 90% in your mathematics test and not 100%, and then made you believe that their actions were OK.

If it was not at school, it was at home. For that reason, I vowed never to tell a soul about the flashback.

Never tell…

As I got older, the feelings of me against the world got stronger. I carried the weight of my greatest pains on my shoulders. I spent many years learning to deal with the pangs of life alone because, in my mind, that is how it was meant to be. My defensive aggressive attitude towards Amai did not cause impact. All the same, this attitude had become my way of coping for many years after that. Still, I vowed never to tell.

Never tell...

Boarding school

At the age of seven
My smile would reach the heavens.
My laugh filled the room.
I talked much,
my name appeared on every prefect's noisemakers' list.

I loved to play under the gum trees.
I would look up searching for snakes.
I knew that when the thunderstorms came
And lightning struck,
The snakes would hide
In the gum trees which were my shade.

I was adventurous, daring and fearless.
Cheerful and lighthearted.

Prose of The Travelling Soul

Curious as any child at seven.

As time passed

I got older,

My lively presence would soon fade.

Slowly ebbing my soul.

Snatching my joy,

As his thick white rope whipped my back.

The teacher kept it specifically for noisemakers.

Snatching my joy,

As her cane would thrash my hands forty-one times.

The teacher was angry

My essay had one word spelled wrong.

As she released me from her soothing hug.

My sister held my swollen hands

Reminded me once again,

I was okay.

But when she moved on to secondary school,
Slowly, my cheerful soul sunk
Into a melancholic song.
I was keen to please.
I stopped talking,
I stopped playing,
I didn't smile.

Still, I forgot to say thank you to the teacher.
How could I dare to be so ungrateful?
A bad child.
Kneeling at the feet of the headmaster
I begged for pardon,
Whilst the others watched.
My body burnt with shame.

Snatching my joy
As his hose pipe struck.

Prose of The Travelling Soul

This time I cannot remember why.
But it was because I was bad.
Some children can't be fixed, they said.
The last day of boarding school
The best day.
I was not sorry I was alive.
I didn't let them hear my heart
Singing songs of joy.

Longing

I longed to touch the sky's blue,
Kiss the stars' silk,
Feel the moon's radiance.
In the night, its silence.

Yet I feared if I let go,
I would fall.
I would fall deep into the darkness that
I would not be able to find my way back up again.

I closed my eyes and I dreamed a dream.
My Lord wrapped me
In sweet embraces of His love,
To keep my mind sound.

The writing

In the expressive writing and reflections, my intention is not to cast blame or to tell on others, but to comprehend the events that occurred (according to my version) and how I have been shaped through them.

Experience thus far has made me realise that we are the drivers of our own journeys, and we are responsible for the paths we choose to take. We cannot control or change how people behave towards us or what will happen to us, but we can choose how we react to it. Although sometimes, if not most of the time (the latter is true for me), we may make the wrong choices. Once we are aware of this, we can acknowledge that these are life lessons and in turn choose to learn from them.

If often, you are not in control

Know that oftentimes, you have a choice.

That said, I do not forget that possibly through anger, confusion, or merely through the imperfection of my soul, I too have intentionally or unintentionally hurt or caused others pain. From the bottom of my heart, I ask for forgiveness. May the Almighty pardon our wrongdoings. May He relieve us of our hardships. Ameen.

The Anger

Eleven to fourteen years of age,
The ache in my chest remained.
To keep my pains restrained.
The persistent sting in my throat,
held my tears back.

Hold onto it,
Don't let go.

Hold on with every strength you can master.
With the pain you feel with every tendon in your muscles.
With the sharp electric cricks you feel in every fibre of your nerves.

Scream, if you must,
But hold on.

And don't let go.

At 15 years old, leaving home,
I said goodbye to everything I knew.
The people I loved and friends I knew.
The culture I did not know then that I loved.
I left Amai,
I said goodbye,
took my demons with me and,
followed my sister and my mother
To embrace a new culture in the west.

Adopting a new culture, new people, I had arrived during the best time of the year. Inhaling the fresh, crisp December air, exploring the busy streets and bright shops, I had never seen so many Christmas lights and trees in one place. The best parts were bright, beautiful and sparkled. All the bad I felt disappeared for that season. The journey I was embarking on, concealed the pain and the hurt briefly whilst I adjusted to the new life, and got my bearings together. It was not long until the affairs of my sleeps returned and I couldn't break away. The one way to describe the effects of the affairs of my sleeps, was the unchanging chaos in my heart, anxiety in my chest and the extreme fear and detestation I felt towards myself. The chronic ache in my chest reappeared. It was a pain I cannot describe but it kept the anger surviving. Anything was a trigger for it; being alone in itself, a reflection of myself in the mirror, I would see Chizero. I preferred to be at school because at least I was occupied with books, teachers, lessons and friends. That meant I could not hear my thoughts, I could not feel anything and I did not have a reason to react. For me, being at school felt good and the teachers were kind.

My mind is enervated beyond doubt.

I feel broken. Repair surpasses.

I can't breathe and I'm burned out.

How did I get here?

Self-love has never lived here.

If it did, I cannot remember.

If love exists, I cannot feel it.

I would not know what to look for.

I feel alone.

The silence.

It makes me feel everything.

Everything that was ever done.

It makes me hear everything.

Everything that was ever said.

I wish I could sleep... forever!!!

At home, if I ever set loose the anger, I don't remember my sister falling victim. She was the one who seemed to bring me comfort and everything felt easy around her. If anyone asked me how I was doing, I would be fine but if my sister asked me, it was like opening Pandora's box. I'm not sure why but I have always felt safe... and wanted when I am with my sister. I don't believe this connection is simply because we are sisters. It is possibly, more than the trials' life has thrown at us. There is something about my sister and her beautiful heart. When her journey redirected her back to the place we once dwelled, I missed her. I hope she knows I love her.

A home we once dwelled,

A zone that had been my comfort,

had now become a place

I feared to return.

My quest for abundance began.

I loved my sister,

Though my fear of Amai,

the previous life I'd had was greater.

My sister returned,

I hope she knows I love her.

The family

After my sister left, I had been living alone for a while. I had wonderful friends. Their beautiful characters, the generosity that I received from their families was my ray of hope that I would be okay. One day, I would look at my reflection and I would be at peace with it. One day, those hurts, I would overcome. Literally life to me proved arduous.

I was used to living alone. While I enjoyed time to myself, I had become tired of living by myself. I didn't take annual leave from work because I felt that I had nobody to spend my holidays with. There was a sense of shame that came with being alone. I craved for human connection a lot of the time. So much so that I would reserve a spot in my life for anyone who showed any form of interest in me, even if their intentions were opportunistic.

Be that as it may, I had a family… the family. If I was in any kind of trouble, if I needed any form of help or somebody to talk to, I would always find it at my place of work. There was, without fail, someone from the family who would be there to support me for most things, if not everything.

I smile as I look back remembering the family particularly the arguments, the hot-headed debates which were almost always taken personally on my part, and the never-ending talks about the ins and outs of each other's personal lives. Despite this, there was a lot more unity, hard work and a huge amount of support for each other. The family was where we all came together. It was the place where this unity would turn to love as we all became a part of each other's lives.

I'm sad to say, on my last day of work, I didn't leave things on good terms with some members of the family. I felt like my journey had taken quite a dramatic turn. One which I felt nobody could comprehend. I suppose I felt hurt by the response and behaviour of others other than the family hitherto, that I did not take time to acknowledge the consequences of my own actions.

Amina G

I contemplate on most days.
The day on which I left the family.
I had caused the winds to blow strong.
Though in my mind, a silent storm.

Perhaps, one or two of them,
members of the family.
Their upset, a result of my doing,
Was enough to curse
My shattered heart Into conflict.

Apprised of their anger,
Fear of the repercussions
of begging pardon,
Was greater than strength to make amends.

"I'm sorry."
It seems easy to say.

Yet there is much strength these words carry.
Peace and comfort they bear plenty.

Had I acknowledged this surely,
I would have been brave
Long before I left the family.

" I'm sorry."
Powerful in its brevity.

To the family

Thank you for being there,
When you didn't need to be.
Thank you for your support,
Your helping hands.
Through God,
You relieved a little of my anxiety.

Brought solace during the loneliest and most desperate times.
When life looked bleak.
You were the family,
but you were my family for the best part.
Thank you

To the family I hurt

I'm sorry I hurt you.
Made you angry.
I caused you pain.
I did not apologise when I should have done.
I could have made half the hurts go away.

You were my family for the best part.
I'm sorry.

To the family

I will always remember

The support

The help

The love

How can I forget?

You were my family for the best part.

Social media

I was able to reconnect with my family who were far away and long-lost via social media. My sister had given me details of some contacts. In communicating with my family through Facebook and WhatsApp, I was reminded that it was not all as bad as I had believed. I was loved. I was wanted. I had some good memories of my uncles and my aunts. I had had grandparents who loved me. They had cared for me. My uncles visited me a lot when I was at boarding school. In the village where my grandparents had lived, they used to take me out a lot, driving through the dusty roads around the village. We drove to a lot of different places. I would sit on my uncle's lap, whichever of them who was driving so that it looked like I was the one driving. One of my uncles had just got married and I spent some time with him and his wife. She loved me like I was her own. My father's sister, my aunt, often came to our house to pick me up and take me to spend the school holidays at her house. I played with my cousin who was of similar age. We had lots of childhood fun. My uncles and aunts spend a lot of their time with me. I remembered that, before building castles in the air, before the flashback, I was loved.

The guidance

Reflecting on the state of my affairs in those days, the spirit of my heart and my mind before the guidance, I remember it like it was yesterday. I can still feel what I was feeling back then. The pain, the sadness, anxiety and fear made me struggle to keep my head whilst I was also struggling to keep my head above water. Everything in my life had become completely unpalatable. During that same time, I had a debate with a brother, in regards to the issue about hell. It may sound peculiar as to why the issue of hell would be up for discussion, though I used to ponder a lot about the reality of this world. I felt that there is too much pain, heartbreak and loss to deal with. The pain that we as human beings afflict on each other as well as ourselves felt overmuch to bear. As much as I feel I have acquired a generous amount of knowledge to assist me to handle it better these days, I can never understand why we find this ideology of wars, destruction and oppression a necessity. Then we pass it onto future generations. I had become extremely fearful of the human being. Of what I could be capable of. My heart shot into a chaos I couldn't explain, the affairs of my sleeps had been getting worse. I was battling with my mind, I would envision things I couldn't describe. I guess it is the description of someone who was at the brink of madness. The fear had somehow made me believe that this world surely was hell; the pain, the hurt, the grief, the loss, illnesses, the distractions and everything else that comes with it. Surely, the suffering we experience in this world; in this life, had to be our hell. So, that is what I told him. I told him that I thought this world was our hell. When we all left this world, we would all go to a better place. We would all go to heaven. A lot of things didn't make sense to me, I had tried a several times to find the right place of worship, where I felt comfortable, and yet I always came out feeling more fearful than before, feeling mixed emotions.

Going over this again, I can see why he would have laughed. Not because he found it funny, merely because it clearly appears to be irrational, as was my state of mind then. Absolute madness. He explained that God has given free will to all of us, we are all able to make choices. We can make a choice to do good or to do bad, to be good people or to be bad people. God has told us that nobody carries the burden of another hence, if this world was our hell, how can it be that we carry the burdens of the bad things that other people do? How can we suffer on this earth for the sins of others? Hell and Paradise do exist, but they exist in the next life. As a result, people have to be accountable for the things they have done in this world. God has told us that there will be a judgement day and everyone will be judged according to the good or bad which they have earned in this world. The explanation he gave me had me shifting my perception of things and, reflecting about our Creator. It relieved a little of the aches and pains in my heart and to my surprise, I slept better that night for the first time in a long time although I knew, I still had a long way to go.

After the explanation, he recommended a book which unbeknownst to me, would redirect my journey to a completely different path. This book would make my heart content and by His mercy, take me on a journey where I would find peace and solace.

At first, I couldn't find the book; Purification of the Heart, a translation & commentary of Imam Al-Mawlud's Matharat Al-Qulub by Sheikh Hamza Yusuf (which I still reread to this day) anywhere to order or to buy. Fortunately, I was able to get hold of some recorded lectures based on the book and also, taught by the author. I listened religiously until I was able to buy it.

From reading the excerpt of the introduction at the back of the book, I knew it had the answers I had been looking for. All those nights I had cried to God and begged Him to take me or to provide for me a solution for my broken life. A way to deal with the pains of this world. And here in my hand, God was giving me the answers I needed.

"My Lord heard me. He knew. All this time, He was listening," I thought to myself as I held this book in my hand.

IF WE EXAMINE THE TRIALS AND TRIBULATIONS ALL OVER THE EARTH, WE'LL FIND THEY ARE ROOTED IN HUMAN HEARTS. Covetousness, the desire to aggress and exploit, the longing to pilfer natural resources, the inordinate love of wealth, and other maladies manifestations of diseases found nowhere but in the heart. Every criminal, miser, abuser, scoffer, embezzler, and hateful person does what he or she does because of a diseased heart. So if you want to change our world, do not begin by rectifying the outward. Instead, change the condition of the inward. It is from the unseen world that the phenomenal world emerges, and it is from the unseen realm of our hearts that all actions spring… We of the modern world are reluctant to ask ourselves –"Why do they occur?" And if we ask that with sincerity, the answer will come back in no uncertain terms: all of this is from our own selves. This is the only empowering position we can take.

-Excerpt from Hamza Yusuf's Introduction

In the book, as we can read from the title, Sheikh

Hamza Yusuf stresses the importance of the condition of the heart in spiritual terms. He states that in the Islamic tradition, the spiritual heart is centred in the physical. Moreover, he gives a lot of references from the Qur'an as well as Hadith and Sunnah of the Prophet of Islam (peace be upon him), that prove that if the heart is not sound then the whole body will not be sound. Particularly on the day of judgement according to the Qur'an, it is the day when neither wealth nor children shall be of benefit [to anyone], except one who comes to God with a sound heart (Qur'an 26: 88-89). God refers to those who have sound hearts as characters that are strong and lack flaws in their spirituality.

Man was truly created anxious (Qur'an 70:19). The heart is easily susceptible to anxiety and agitation. Not so those who pray and are constant in their prayers (Qur'an 70: 22-23). Those who pray with a humble and open heart connected with God the Almighty, the Creator of all. Those whose hearts are constant in the remembrance of God. Who remember God standing, sitting, and lying down (Qur'an 3: 191)

This book altogether changed my life. I did not know anything else but to reach out to my Lord. I prayed for guidance. I was gifted with the Quran, the Divine book that would heal my completely broken and damaged heart. There were other books too, such as; The beginning of Guidance by Abu Hamid Al Ghazali translated by Mashhad Al-Allaf, as well as a book of prayers. I was advised that in order to have clarity of the Quran, one had to study the Hadith and Sunnah of Prophet Muhammad (peace be upon him) as well. I spend a lot of time reading and researching about Islam. Although I knew that I had to submit fully to God, I had to become a Muslim, I was letting time pass me by as I dipped my hands into this religion that was new to me but was always alive.

Is it that this love I long for, does not exist.

Was it ever. Will it never be. Or,
Could it be that this love,
Lives within the heart and with the Creator.
Then, this love is
A love without end.

"Take benefit of five before five ;

Your youth before old age
Your health before sickness
Your wealth before poverty
Your free time before preoccupation
Your life before death."
Prophet Muhammad (peace be upon him)

"Your life before death."

In the midst of my daily studying about the religion

of Islam, I came across the above Hadith of the Prophet Muhammad. It moved something in my heart. I read over and I read it again. Then I read the last benefit more. It was there in black and white but my eyes saw it in bold black and white. "Your life before death."

Death is inevitable. It is true. That was the moment I decided to change my life.

Allah. Islam & Muslims. The Qur'an. Prophet Muhammad (pbuh)

Sources used:

Vision of Islam by Sachiko Murata & William C Chittick. Qur'an, a new translation by M.A.S Abdel Haleem.

Allah is the Arabic name for God, although it means the ONE God, it is referring to Allah as one and alone. He has no partners, he did not beget nor was he begotten. Nothing is comparable to Him. Quran 112: 1-4

When people hear this word, they naturally think that it means that Muslims believe in a god, Allah, just as the ancient Greeks believed in Zeus, many Hindus believe in Vishnu, and every tribe has its own god. To think of Allah in these terms is to imply that the Jews and/or Christians believe in the real God, but Muslims have their own local god, or a false idea about God.

In Arabic, Allah simply means "God." The Koran, the Hadith, and the whole Islamic tradition maintain that the God of the Jews, the Christians, and the Muslims is a single God. Arabic-speaking Muslims cannot imagine using a different word than Allah when referring to the God worshipped by Christians and Jews. Arabic-speaking Christians and Jews worship God using the word Allah.

Vision of Islam — Sachiko Murata & William C Chittick

Islam is an Arabic word which means "submission to God's will". It is a religion which was confirmed by the Quran and Prophet Muhammad (peace be upon him) through the angel Gabriel (Jibril in Arabic).

A Muslim is one who has submitted to God's will, to the religion of Islam. One who has submitted to a way of life according to God's will.

The Qur'an is the Divine book of guidance and truth which Muslims read and recite every day. Muslims believe that the Holy Qur'an is the word of God which was given to Prophet Muhammad through the archangel Gabriel.

This is the book, in it is guidance sure, without doubt to those who are mindful of God, who believe in the unseen, are steadfast in prayer, and spend out of what We have provided for them; those who believe in the revelation sent to you (Muhammad) and in what was sent before you and (in their hearts) have the assurance of the Hereafter. They are on (true guidance, from their Lord and it is those who will prosper. Qur'an 2: 2-5

Those who believe in the revelation sent to you (Muhammad) and in what was sent before you. Qur'an 2:4

This verse is referring to all of God's messengers (including Moses and Jesus, peace be upon them) and the Holy books; the Tawrah (Torah), the Injil (Bible) and the Qur'an.

Muslims live their daily lives by the Qur'an. It is the origin for all matters such as spiritual, financial, rightfulness and a means of keeping the body and soul together. That is to say, the entire religious life of a Muslim is based on the Qur'an, the Divine book.

If you want to understand the Muslim and their religion, you have to study the Hadith and the sunna of the Prophet Muhammad (peace be upon him) as well as his seerah. The Hadith is a record of sayings of Prophet Muhammad (peace be upon him) which is consecrated and recognised as a significant source of religious law next to the Qur'an. The narrators were his companions and followers who were present at the time of the Prophet Muhammad (peace be upon him). The tradition and practice, which is the sunna itself at the time would also be indicated.

The seerah in simple terms is the biography of a person's life. In this instance, we would study the life and journey of the Prophet Muhammad (peace be upon him). There is a book which in my opinion tells in great detail of the Prophet's life (peace be upon him) written by Martin Lings entitled MUHAMMAD. It tells through and through, methodically and thoroughly the life of Prophet Muhammad (peace be upon him), before and after the revelation up until the end of his life. Prophet Muhammad (peace be upon him) was a messenger of God who was called to warn and spread the message of God to his community and the whole of mankind. As Muslims, we believe he was a mercy for mankind.

Prophet Muhammad, peace and blessings upon him

Our master,

He was the last of God's messengers.

Kind, patient,

He was forgiving.

He visited those who were sick,

Even if they didn't like him.

He still cared for their health

He would still pray for them.

An example is the story of the woman who used to throw filth and rubbish at the Prophet whenever he would pass her house. One day, he noticed her absence and asked after her. When he learnt that she was sick, he visited her. She was so surprised by his compassion and kindness that she embraced Islam.

He taught mankind to respect their elders
Take care of their parents.
Honour your mother, your mother, your mother,
Your paradise lies under her feet.
Honour your father.

Al-Amīn, one of his beautiful names, he was given.
He was honest and trustworthy.
He was fair and just in all his dealings.
He helped the poor and fed the hungry.
He cared for the orphans and the widows.
He taught mankind to be gentle and loving to children,
Your daughters are your doors to paradise.
He loved animals and nature.

He taught mankind
The strongest man is not the one who can hold his fist in a fight,

But the one who holds himself when he is angry.

Prophet Muhammad, peace and blessings upon him.

Truly he was a mercy for mankind.

His prayers and tears for us

He prayed for our guidance.

Firm in his faith.

May we always seek to learn more about who he was.

May our prayers always be for him.

Peace and blessings upon him, our master.

Islam

Islam,

the religion of peace.

With it,

Brings the Qur'an (The Divine Book),

The actions and sayings of the Prophet Muhammad

(Peace and blessings upon him).

And the message he brought forth.

Islam,

A faith once breathed into the heart,

Gives you a new start.

The spirits of the walking dead depart.

A way of life that teaches beautiful patience,

A peaceful happiness.

Prophet Muhammad, he was a mercy for mankind.

The Divine Book, a healing for mankind.

It reminds us of God's compassion.

The book of miracles, it breaks the shackles that bind us to misery.

To God belongs all Glory.

Islam,

A way of life, a religion

That mended my crushed soul.

Relieved my fears, and taught me

Only He has Control.

Taught me to worship Him,

To do better, to be better.

Entering Paradise,

My only goal.

Islam,

A religion that saved my wretched soul.

Becoming Muslim

The day,

A beautiful Sunday morning.

The sun gleamed through the windows

Of my lonely and small apartment.

A glimmer of hope.

As I read the email from the Sheikh,

He had time to meet me,

My heart burst out beats of joy.

This was the day,

A beautiful bright spring Sunday.

Becoming Muslim,

I needed support.

The brothers and the sister,

Her child safely fastened in her car seat.

They put their plans aside

To support me.
Their generosity, Their kindness
Will forever hold a place
In my heart.

We drove to meet the Sheikh.
As we got closer,
My pains slowly giving way.
Becoming Muslim
Would break the shackles
That kept me chained to despair.

The Sheikh,
The brothers and sisters,
Uncles and aunts,
The sister, with her beautiful child.
I'll always be grateful,
Their support.

May God bless them.

Becoming Muslim
It was the beginning
Of my journey
To healing.

The Cradle of life

Ash hadhu anla ilaha illalahu wa ash hadhu ana Muhammadu arasoolullah.

I bear witness that there is no god but God and I bear witness that Muhammad is the messenger of Allah.

In the moment that I said the declaration, I felt as though the words were running through me as blood runs through the body. My life was being renewed afresh. Everything past and present turned. My perception of life, people, religion, of events, of negative and positive and of myself had been transformed.

I couldn't comprehend the divinity of the words I had just uttered. I didn't have full knowledge of the religion of Islam and I didn't have all the answers and yet, I knew it was the right path on my journey. Unsurprisingly, Islam is a way of life that requires one to constantly seek knowledge and guidance. It is a life of endless learning. It brings contentment to the heart. Contentment, happiness, abundance and success; all of which I had been seeking all my life. Spiritually and mentally, I had travelled far and wide for this. I had sought it in others and expected it from others. I had given everything I had and adapted myself to other people's standards in order to find it. For all that, I came to nothing but spiritual emptiness and pain. When I found Islam, I found everything and more. I was born again. It was the cradle of my life.

The shahada, the declaration.

As it flowed through my whole being,

Declaring the oneness of God, and the Prophethood of Muhammad (peace and blessings upon him),

Our master.

I pledged to my Lord,

I would uphold His covenant and His promise

To the best of my ability.

I would submit to His will.

Amina G

I would live according to His will
To the best of my ability.
I would do my best to help those in need
Be kind to my neighbours.
I would remember my responsibilities
In my community,
In society.
I pledged to my Lord,
I would fast during the Holy month of Ramadan.
I would give a part of my earnings if I am able,
To those who need it most
Whilst reminding myself first that charity,
It begins at home.

I pledged to my Lord,
By his will, I would make the pilgrimage to Mecca
In the first ten days of Dhu al-Hijjah.

The five pillars I pledged to my Lord,

I would live according to His will

To the very best of my ability.

Amina G

The hardest I've ever Learned…

When I used to love, I loved wholeheartedly.

I gave everything I had,

I loved with everything I had, everything I was.

I would walk to the end of the world and back again.

Nothing was more important.

When I used to love, I loved too much,

I said too much.

Until I was broken, with nothing left to give

Empty hands… Cracked.

The creation,

It doesn't matter how much you love them, or how much they love you.

The creation will always fall short

Even if, they don't mean to.

We were by human nature created imperfect after all.

The Creator,

The Creator will never fall short.

He will never break you.

Love Him wholeheartedly,

With everything you are.

Give Him everything you have.

Walk to the end of the world, for Him.

Love Him every day.

Richly, each day.

More than anyone

This is the hardest lesson I've ever learnt.

I would bring it all back

If I could turn back time for you,

If I could bring back those times,

Those moments when you were sad, confused, lost and frightened.

Those times when you felt neglected, rejected

Again, and again.

When you felt lonely like nobody loved you.

If I could bring back those times back when you were happy.

When you felt so much joy that the tiniest thought of its disappearance

Brought sadness to your heart.

If I could bring it all back, I would.

I would bring it all back so I could tell you,

I'm here, you are safe.

Prose of The Travelling Soul

You are enough just as you are.
The happiness which you feel,
you are deserving of it.
The love which you feel, it's true,
You are loved, I love you.
It's all yours
You are where need to be
Home
Safe

I would bring it all back,
For you.

In Islam, we believe that we are all born as Muslims. This means that we are all born submissive to the will of God. Another is that before the whole of the creation was brought to earth, that is to say, before we were all born, we bore witness that God is our Lord and there is none other than Him.

(Prophet), when Your Lord took out the offspring from the loins of the Children of Adam and made them bear witness about themselves, He said, 'Am I not your Lord?' and they replied, 'Yes, we bear witness.' Qur'an 7: 172.

This covenant that God took from us has not been erased from our memories. It is a natural inclination which is instilled in our hearts and souls and drives us to believe in God and long to know Him.

Ibn Qutaybah (may God be pleased with him) who was an Islamic scholar of Persian origin said:

What is meant by the words of the hadith, "Every newborn is born in a state of fitrah (natural inclination)," refers to the covenant that Allah took from them when they were in the loins of their father Adam, "and made them testify concerning themselves (saying): 'Am I not your Lord?' They said: 'Yes'" (Qur'an 7: 172)

I had always felt something was missing in my life. I believed in God although I didn't have a spiritual connection with God. So, when I became a Muslim, I returned to submitting myself to the will of God. I turned back to God. Most would say I reverted.

This is what you were promised- this is for everyone who turned often to God and kept Him in mind, who held the most gracious awe, though He is unseen, who comes before Him with a heart turned to Him in devotion. Qur'an 50: 32-33.

At first, I didn't tell my friends, work colleagues or family. I had not thought through the seriousness of my decision of which I truly believed was the right choice for me. Albeit, some found out before I could tell them.

The Prophet (peace be upon him) said, "Islam came to the world as something strange, and it will also leave the world as something strange." That said, some had questions regarding the religion. Plenty of which I couldn't answer. Others had information to share with me. Bad things that other Muslims had done. Bad mistakes Muslims had made. Some did their best to instil fear of Islam and Muslims in the hope that I would denounce the religion. When I stood firm in my faith, I was amazed at how the religion of Islam could fill my heart with genuine; real hope, induce contentment whilst at the same time, drastically changing the atmosphere that was in my surroundings. My heart had felt emptiness for a long time. Regardless, I searched for answers to the questions which had been so dubiously thrown at me and on the lonely days, I cried to my Lord. I realised that in the end, it was all in my favour.

Perhaps you hate a thing and it is good for you; and perhaps you love a thing and it is bad for you. Allah knows, while you know not. Qur'an 2:216

Although my family did not agree with my decision, all praises are for God, they were accepting as they could see the positive changes.

True Islam is perfect,

Muslims are not perfect.

For they are human beings like you.

If a Muslim makes a mistake or commits a crime,

Blame the individual

Not the whole ummah (all Muslims).

Blame the individual

Not the religion.

In spite of the nepotism from the very few which

may have been minor although caused me a lot of anxiety at times, it was not at all bad. There is a certain comfort and calm felt in holding tight to the rope of God.

Whoever holds fast to God will be guided to the straight path. Qur'an 3:101

I'm home

You have placed hope in my heart
To survive the fears I feel, and the hurts I endure
To hold firm in my faith.
Through this, I will toil
Until I'm home,
Finally safe.

Safe,
Because it was only ever You
It has always been You
It will always be You
Ya Rabb, my Lord!
I'm Home.

With You, I have everything

They don't know how much it all hurts

They could never comprehend the affairs of my sleeps

They don't know how much this broken and wrecked heart,

Longs for healing, peace, and solace in Your promise

They gossip

They laugh

They curse

For speculation tells them

I am now somebody to be feared

As if I may cause them harm

They don't know

Their words and curses are more raw than sticks and stones

Wounds may heal

But scars will remain

An aide-mémoire of pain once inflicted

My Lord

They don't know

With You, I have everything.

My first month of Ramadan

That year, I would fast for the first time. Only a few weeks after I converted to Islam. The month of Ramadan when all Muslims fast for thirty days because God has instructed those who submit to Him to do so.

It was in the month of Ramadan that the Qur'an was revealed as guidance for mankind, clear messages giving guidance and distinguishing between right and wrong. So any one of you who sees in that month should fast, and anyone who is ill or on a journey should make up for the lost days by fasting on other days later. God wants ease for you, not hardship. He wants you to complete the prescribed period and to glorify Him for having guided you, so that you may be thankful. Qur'an 2:185

Truth be told, I had never fasted for a day in my life, not even half a day let alone for 30 days. I was anxious. I wasn't sure if I would've been able to do it. As I look back, I realise that that month brought me blessings multiplied, all praises are for God. There are many blessings that come with the month itself although being a revert, sincerely trying your best, is more rewarding as God says he gives more to those who find it a challenge but still try.

I was able to fast for the whole month, despite missing suhoor (the meal which is eaten just before the dawn prayer during the fasting days), all praises are for God. This was due to the fact that I was not aware I had to get up and eat before the dawn prayer. If I was told about it, perhaps I didn't understand.

If fasting is something new not just to you but also to those around you, it will most certainly be perceived as weird. Some will let you be, others will talk and ask questions; which is natural. Still, there are those who may take it very badly. It might be that they love you, which makes it reasonable as it would be out of concern. In a world where fasting is seldom, it is judged as extremely boring, unhealthy and unfitting in society; all of which are far from the truth. I was now spending a lot of my time reading, connecting with the Quran and praying whilst they had barbecues outside, ate and drank merrily into the sunset. It is wonderful to celebrate the sunshine, the butterflies and the fresh air. I would have been keen to join, but my life had taken such a drastic turn. That in itself was incongruous and out of the blue. It was mind-bending for some to apply logic to my questionable behaviour. How could they understand when in truth, they truly didn't know my deepest secrets, my anxieties and my fears. I had, after all, vowed never to tell, or open my heart to anyone and so, I dealt with "stuff" on my own, in my own head. I don't blame them for their misknowledge although I wonder if they had known, would they have been able to appreciate this sudden turn. Would they have been able to feel the light-heartedness that I was feeling or, hear the songs of tranquillity in my heart? God mentions in the Qur'an, that even if He was to produce more proof (and He has in many ways) of

His existence, they will still not believe. That considered, how can I expect others to appreciate the reasoning behind my turning?

Even if We had sent the angels down to them (with the message), and the dead spoke to them (of it), and We gathered together every (created) thing in front of them, they still would not believe, unless God should will it. But most of them, (of that), are ignorant. Qur'an 6:111

The main purpose behind Ramadan is the struggle. The struggle against one's soul to abstain from everything until sunset. Besides food and drink, it is the struggle to remove oneself from bad habits such as idle talk, gossiping, being angry, hurting others, greed etc. It is an opportunity to connect with God on a spiritual level, to do good deeds and form good habits with yourself and others. It is a time to empty the soul of sins and change the heart, God willing. It is also a time to recognise the struggles of others, help them if you are able to and pray for them as well as praying for the Prophet Muhammad (peace be upon him). There are many invisible blessings that come with Ramadan in particular for those who reflect with understanding. The connection with the month of Ramadan on a spiritual level is never always the same. Sometimes the struggle is bittersweet, glory to God and other times, it seems to flow swiftly, all praises are for God.

There were a lot of times during my first Ramadan when I experienced intense loneliness. I felt bullied into a corner, my eyes filled with silent tears of defeat. There were many questions to which I didn't have immediate answers. It was my most desolate month of fasting and yet it was also the best month of fasting where I felt more connected with God. It was hard although I believe God brought ease with it, over and above. Almost every day of the month, I had an invitation to break fast with other Muslims and on some nights, I was taking part in Taraweeh prayers. Taraweeh prayers are additional ritual prayers performed after the obligatory night prayers during the month of Ramadan. I also spend some weekends with other Muslims until it was time to break fast, and we ate together. I was able to make contact when my surroundings got too challenging. God gave me that ray of hope in my personal struggles.

So truly where there is hardship there is also ease. Qur'an 94:5

Dear Ramadan

You entered into my life

For the first time

You came too soon

I was unprepared

Perhaps you knew

About the mess in my head

And the turmoil in my heart

Perhaps you'd heard

The silent screams

And saw the tears on my pillow

Amina G

Dear Ramadan
When you came
I did not know the gift
You would bring with you
For I had never
Not even half a day
Let alone a day in my life
Had a taste of you

Dear Ramadan
You have taught me
Plenty of which I did not know
You have opened my mind
To many things I had not appreciated
You have shown me
I have strength I did not know I had
You have taught me
What it means to be patient

That in the struggle there is ease Mercy
A strange calmness And comfort

Dear Ramadan
Slowly I have come to understand a little of myself
Dismantling the walls around myself
Which I had spent years building

Dear Ramadan
You reminded me to reflect
On the message
On the signs
Every day, You reminded me of our Lord
Dear Ramadan
Thank you for stopping by
I'm sad you are leaving
I will remember the lessons
You have taught me

Amina G

Dear Ramadan

I pray if God wills it

We will meet again soon

Be on your way

With love

To the broken hearts

My dearest ones,
Your Lord has not forsaken you.
He has heard your silent cries.
He sees your tears.
He knows your pain.
With Him, nothing goes in vain.

Raise your hands,
reach out to your Lord.
He will never leave you.
He has not left you.
He is nearer to you than your jugular vein.

My dearest ones,
I write this to you… for you.
I pray our Lord, our Helper,

will relieve you of your burdens.

Release the troubles that live within your soul.

My dearest ones,

Know that nothing lasts forever.

This pain, this grief you feel today,

will be gone tomorrow.

And if it stays any longer,

it will get easier.

So, don't give up hope.

I pray that one day,

Our Lord will free our souls.

One day, you will be able to find peace and comfort

In Him.

My dearest ones,

I say a prayer for you often.

May our Lord remove the pains that have left you feeling broken.

Allah

The greatest name

The All Divine

Cause of all existence

You have known me, even before You created me.

You know what I do not know.

You have heard my cries

You have seen what nobody else has seen.

My existence, my deeds are nothing without you.

You are the reason I live.

Allahu Akbar, Allah is the Greatest.

Prophet Muhammad (peace be upon him) said, "Allah has ninety-nine names, that is one hundred minus one, and whoever knows them will go to Paradise." (The Sahih Bukhari collection of Hadiths)

Abu Hurairah who was one of the companions of Prophet Muhammad (peace be upon him), reported him as saying, "Verily there are ninety-nine names for Allah, that is excepting one. He who enumerates them would get into Paradise." (Sahih Muslim collection of Hadiths)

Allah- there is no deity except Him. To Him belong the best names.

Qur'an 20: 8

The Most Beautiful Names Belong to Allah, so call on Him by Them.

Qur'an 7: 180

The best and most beautiful names of God

Asmaa'ul Husna. The best and most beautiful names (Reflecting on the 99 beautiful names of God, includes Islamic prayers and verses from the Qur'an. Please note that the names are not in their original order).

They asked me who I loved, so I gave them 99 names
-author unknown

Ar-Rahman, The Compassionate

Ar-Rahīm, The Most Merciful

I have failed over and over. I have stewed in my own despair, loss and grief. But Your compassion and forgiveness continues to be.

I am surrounded by your mercy. Your Mercy I hold within.

Al-Quddus, The Holy One who is free from all blemishes

I have fallen in error, over and over but You continue to show me the way.

Al-Malik, The King, The Sovereign

Al-'Awwal, The First, The Beginning-less

Al-Ākhir, The Last, The Endless.

You are my Lord, I am your servant. There is no God but You. You are the first and the cause of all that became. There was nothing before You, there is nothing after You. You are the last. The eternal.

As-Salaam, Giver of Peace.

Al-Mu'min, The Guarantor, The Affirming.

Al-Muhaymin, The giver of Protection.

You save me from dangers, some I cannot see. You illuminate the light of faith in my heart, giving me solace. In my loneliness and the fear. In the hunger and the struggle with my soul. In ghusl, I'm cleansed. In sujood, prostration, I'm purified. Your Promise true. The Lord of the straight path.

Al-'Āzīz, The Almighty.

Al-Muqeet, The Nourisher, Giver of Sustenance and Strength.

La Hawla wala quwatta ila Billah. There is no power and no strength except with God.

Al-Jabbār, The Compeller, The Lofty, The Irresistible.

In my brokenness, hurts and unfamiliarity. You put me back together. You enlighten me, the purpose of my pain. O, Al-Jabbār! Increase me in knowledge that is of benefit, a good provision and deeds that will be accepted.

Al-Mutakabbir, The Majestic, The Supreme.

There is a majestic greatness in everything you have created. In Your Supremacy, there are signs for those who reflect and understand.

Al-Khāliq, The Creator.

Al-Bari, The One who gives life.

Al-Musawwir, Fashioner of shapes.

You have created us, all that is on earth and the universe from nothing. Our stories were written before we were. You gave us life, fashioned and moulded us into the most perfect beautiful shapes.

Al-Qahhār, The One who has control over all things.

All of this was not without purpose. Place the love of this world in my hands and the love of the afterlife in my heart.

Thinking of my shame. I cried, " I have a past I cannot change."

Al-Ghaffār, The repeatedly Forgiving, **Al-Ghafūr,** The Much Forgiving replied, "Come. Come to Islam as you are."

I said, "There are some things I cannot speak of."

Al-Aleem, The All-knowing. **Al-Khabeer,** The All-Knowing, All aware said, "Indeed, I know everything. That which is hidden and what you conceal. Come as you are."

Al-Latīf, The Gentle, The Subtly Kind.

My Lord is most subtle in achieving what He will; He is all knowing, the Truly Wise. Qur'an 12:100

As-Sami', The All Hearing asked me, "Why do you scream in silence, when I am watchful?"

He asked, "Why the storm in your heart, when I am nearer to you than your jugular vein?"

I cried, "O! **Al-Basīr,** The One who sees all things, there are things I wish others not to see."

He asked, "Why do you remain in the dark, when there is light in you?"

I replied, "It is fear of exposure. I fear in the light, my load will be on sight."

He said, "Don't you know, your load is of value. It is through exposure that your light will shine."

Cherished with growth and inspiration. I opened my heart to,

Al-Hakam, The Judge.

Al-A'dl, The Utterly Just.

Al-Wahhab, The Giver of all things, The Bestower.

Al-Razzāq, The Sustainer and Provider.

I came to You when I had nothing. You gave me everything.

Al-Fattāh, The remover of difficulties and Giver of decisions.

He asked, "Why do you remain imprisoned by the opinions of others. Your worth you do not need to justify."

I replied, "It is fear of loneliness. In solitude, I fear I might lose my spine."

He said, "Don't you know you are not alone? Even in solitude, it is freedom of the mind."

Al-Qābid, The straightener of Sustenance.

Al-Bāsit, The Extender of Sustenance.

You opened the doors of sustenance and removed my hardship and replaced it with abundance, joy and relief. Alhamdulillah, SubhanAllah wa bihamdihi. All praises are for God. Glory to Him, Praised is He.

Al-Khāfid, The Abaser, The One who Humbles and lowers.

My Lord, put me amongst those who bow in prostration to You. O Allah, I ask You for Your love, and the love of those who love You, and all of the actions that would bring me closer to be loved by You.– Prophet David's supplication (peace be upon him).

Ar-Rāfi, The Exalter.

Al-Mu'iz, The Giver of Honour.

Al-Muzil, The Giver of Dishonour.

We believe in You. We have put our trust in You. There is no God but You. Raise us to honour. Give us honour. Protect us from humiliation.

Al-Halīm, The Forbearing.

Al-Wāsi, The Lenient.

I have been guilty a thousand times and more. Over and over. Still, Your mercy prevails. Your compassion has no end.

Al-Karīm, The Generous, The Bountiful.

Because of Your generosity. I fall to my knees in prostration and beg, in hope of gaining Your forgiveness. Your favours to mankind are endless.

Al-'Azeem, The Great, The Magnificent.

Your Divinity on the earth, below and in the heavens above. Glory be to You. For in the realms where our sight cannot reach and of which our minds cannot envision. There is perfect greatness. Greatness which belongs only to You.

Al-Alīy, The Sublime.

You are the most high.

Al-Kabīr, The most Great.

There is no one greater than You.

Al-Hafīdh, The Preserver

Ash-Shakūr, The Grateful.

Your reward is much greater than anything we could imagine.

Al-Hafeez, The Protector

In my ignorance and eagerness to please others, I placed myself in invisible dangers. You are our protector. You have protected me even when I did not know.

Al-Wadud, The Most Loving.

It is through Your love that is my existence. A love for your servants that can not be compared not even to that of a mother's love for her child.

Al-Haseeb, The bringer of Judgement, The reckoner.

We are accountable to You for our actions. You are sufficient for us. Protect us against the evils of others.

Al-Jalīl, The Glorious, The Lord of Majesty and might.

Glory be to You. There is nothing comparable to You.

Al-Raqīb, The Caretaker, The Watchful

In the terrible decisions I have made when I thought it impossible, You took care of me.

Al-Mujīb, The Responsive, The Answer.

On the days and night that I cried to You, You have answered my prayers in more ways than I could imagine.

Al-Hakīm, The Wise.

Al-Majīd, The Glorious, The Majestic, The Venerable.

When I thought my desires and my worldly needs were good for me. They were lessons to learn. When I thought my pain and trials were bad for me. They were blessings in them. You know best, while we do not. You are pure perfection. There is wisdom in all your actions.

Al-Bā'ith, The Resurrector.

To You, we belong, to You, we shall return. Only You can give life back. You will raise us on Judgement day.

Ash-Shahīd, The Witness.

Al-Haqq, The Truth, The real.

You witness everything that happens everywhere. A truth never unchanged.

Al-Wakīl, The Trustee, The Dependable.

Al-Qawīy, The Strong.

We knock at the doors of Your mercy. Completely depended on You. We are nothing without strength from You. Ya **Al-Matīn,** The Firm, The Steadfast.

Al-Walīy, The Friend, The Patron, The Helper.

Help us to become good characters.

Al-Hamīd, The All Praiseworthy.

Innaka hamīdun majid. Verily You are praiseworthy.

Al-Muhsīy, The Accountor, The Numberer of All.

Al-Mubdi', The Originator, The Initiator.

Al-Mu'īd, The Restorer, The Reinstator Who Brings Back All.

Al-Muhyi, The Giver of Life.

The Originator. You have the power to create again. You are the Giver of life. Heal our diseased, wounded and bleeding hearts. You created death. A death no one else can do. Ya **Al-Mumīt,** The Bringer of death.

Al-Hayy, The Living, The Ever-Lasting.

Al-Wāhid, The One, The Unique.

Al-'Ahad, The One Unequalled, The Unity.

As-Samad, The Eternal, The Absolute, The Self-Sufficient.

Al-Bāqīy, The Infinite, The Everlasting.

Qul Huwallahu Ahad. Allahus Samad. Lam ya lid wa lam yulad. Walam yakullahu kufuwan Ahad. Say He is One. The Eternal. He does not beget nor is He begotten. Nothing is comparable to Him. Qur'an 112: 1-4

Creation and time will end. But You are eternal, everlasting and You will exist forever. You were alive… are alive… and You will remain alive.

Al-Qayyūm, The Guardian, The Sustainer of life.

The sustainer of all that exists. We seek refuge in you from weakness and laziness. You are our Protector, Who continuously Provides.

Ya Hayyul Qayyum! O Ever-Living, Sustainer of all. I besiege Your Mercy. Correct all of my affairs and, do not leave me to my soul, even for a blink of an eye.

— Prophet Muhammad's (peace be upon him) supplication.

Al-Wājid, The Finder, The unfailing.

May the food you provide for us be a source of strength and nourishment for us. The guidance You give illuminate and kindle the light in our hearts.

Al-Qādir, The All Powerful, The Omnipotent One

Al-Muqtadir, The Powerful.

You create power and dominate power over all. You have full power over all. You are the Supreme, The Most High.

Al-Muqaddim, He who brings Forward, who causes advancement.

In my sciolism, You have directed my life to knowing You. Give us success in this life and the next. Give us the good of this world, and the good of the next. Protect us from the punishment of the hellfire.

Al-Mu'akhkhir, The Delayer, He who puts far away.

Az-Zāhir, The Manifest, The Evident.

Al-Bātin, The Hidden, The Unmanifest.

You have bestowed upon us wisdom and reason to know You. Do not leave us to our own selves, even for a blink of an eye. For we come to You with limited minds, understanding little knowledge of Your Divinity.

Al-Muqsit, The Equitable, The Requiter.

You are the sole manager and governor of the whole creation. Increase us in riches for your immeasurable abundance. Increase us in gratuity from You.

O, Al-Muta'ālīy, The Most High, You are far above the attributes of the entire creation.

Al-Bar, The Good.

Al-Muntaqim, The Avenger.

Give us good in this world and good in the Hereafter, and save us from the punishment of the fire. Qur'an 2: 201

At-Tawwāb, The oft Returning.

Al-'Afūw, The One who Pardons.

Ar-Rauf, The Kind.

Itha jaa nasru Allahi waafalthu. Waraayta alnnasa yadkhuloona fee deeni Allahi afwajan. Fasabbih bihamdi rabbika wastaghfirhu innahu kana tawwaba. When God's help comes, and He opens up your way, when you see people embracing God's faith in crowds, celebrate the praise of Your Lord and ask for His forgiveness: He is always ready to accept repentance.

Qur'an110: 1-3

Al-Mālik-ul-Mulk, The owner of all Sovereignty.

Al-Mughnīy, The Enricher.

The Kingdom belongs to You. Grant us wealth, self-sufficiency and independence.

Dhū-l -Jalāli wa-l-ikrām, The Lord of Majesty and Generosity.

Soften our hearts towards those who are suffering. Grant them honour, self-sufficiency. Ameen.

Al-Ghanīy, The Independent.

You are free from need, but we are lost without You. We are lost for we are in great need of You.

I asked my Lord, "Please grant me this and that for I feel it to be good for my soul."

Al-Māni', The Withholder, The Shielder, The defender, replied, "It may be that you dislike something although it is good for you, or you may like something although it is bad for you: God knows and you do not." Qur'an 2: 216

Al-Jāmi', The Assembler.

Lost

Of

Valuable

Energy. From the walking dead, You have given me life. You have shown me the way to;

Lean

On the

Value of the Divine

Energy

Again.

Ad-Dār, One who can cause loss.
Al-Hādīy, The Guide, The Way.

In the guidance to the religion, crushed by the sadness of what I had lost. You gave me everything and more.

"Indeed what is to come will be better for you than what has gone by." Qur'an 93: 4

An-Nāfi, The One who confers Benefits.

Ar-Rasheed, The Guide to the Right Path.

Make us good characters. Implant piety in our hearts, in the depth of our souls.

An-Nur, The Light.

Create light in my heart

And light in my eyes

And light in my hearing

And light on my right

And light on my left

And light above me

And light beneath me

And light in front of me And light behind me And appoint light for me And Magnify light for me

Oh Allah, bestow light upon me

(Prayer of the Prophet (peace be upon him) (Sahih Muslim)

Al-Badi', The Deviser, The Incomparable.

Al-Wārith, The Supporter of All.

With the weight of hardships heavy on us. Puffy eyelids from tears of grief and sorrow. Grant us relief. To You, we belong, to You, we shall return. You are our Protector. Protect us against hardships and calamities.

As-Sabur, The patient, The Most Forbearing.

Time and time again, I have wronged against myself. You are most forbearing. Your patience with us has no comparison.

Rabeel Alamin, Lord of the worlds.

Ruler of judgement day Only You do we ask for help

Only You do we worship

Guide us on the straight path

Not on the path of those who have angered You. Ameen.

Al-Fatiha, The Opening Qur'an 1: 1-7

O Allah, for the sake of Your Beautiful Names and for the sake of the ones whom Your Names are manifest, lead us on their path. Let us see Your attributes everywhere without, and cleanse the mirror of our hearts that perchance we may see Your beauty reflect within. Ameen.

— Du'as for the contentment of the heart.

Poetry and meditation of The heart

ALLAH

Your heart beats for Allah

Every breath

Every beat

It is a calling for Allah

Sit with yourself

Take a moment

Listen to the beat of your heart

Can you hear its call?

ALLAH

ALLAH

ALLAH

If a man knows his heart, he knows himself. If he knows himself, he knows God.

He is prepared for receiving such knowledge only through his heart and not by the means of any other bodily organs. For it is the heart that knows Allah, works for Allah, draws near to Allah and reveals that which is in the presence of Allah. All the other organs are merely followers that the heart uses and employs. For it is the heart that is accepted by Allah when it is free from all except Him, and veiled from Allah when it is totally absorbed in other than Him. The heart is that in which if a man knows it, he knows himself and if he knows himself, he knows his Lord. And it is that which if he knows it not, he knows not himself and if he knows not himself, he knows not his Lord.

Knowledge of the heart and of the true nature of its traits is the root of the religion and the path of the seeker. — Imam Al-Ghazali

Blessed are the pure at heart, for they shall see God. -Jesus (peace be upon him).

Softening of the heart

Water softens everything. It removes impurities. When you soak something that is hard in water, it begins to soften. Perhaps that is why God constantly reminds us to run water over our faces, hands and feet thrice, fives times a day. He tells us to wash our bodies under some circumstances. We are encouraged to drink more water than anything else so that toxins in the body are removed. Perhaps in this act of drinking, washing (wudu and ghusl), it is the beginning of the process to soften the heart.

Treatment of the heart

When one's body is infected with a virus, he does not have the passion to fill his stomach with food and worldly desires. Somehow the body knows not to feed the virus. Removal of desire for food inhibits the virus from nourishment and growth.

This is the same for the treatment of the diseases of the heart. Averting it from excessive worldly desires will inhibit nourishment and growth of its diseases thus avoiding the hardening of the heart.

Black spot

On the human heart is a black spot,
A symbol of imperfection.
Guard it with utmost care,
Your life depends on it.
Turn to the Creator in repentance and reliance,
It will remain polished and unmoved.
Heedlessness, sin and corruption,
The spot will increase in growth.
Immersing the heart with its darkness
Thus hardening the heart.

Surely in the breast of humanity is a lump of flesh. If sound, the whole body is sound, and if corrupt then the whole body is corrupt. Is it not the heart?

— Prophet Muhammad (peace be upon him)

Sinners

Sinners
Breakers of hearts
Send hearts into turmoil
Bleeding

That day, She broke down
Holding on tight to the rope of her Creator
She picked up her shattered heart
From the floor of her kitchen
And put the pieces back together again

Sinners
She said a prayer
For the burdens
They left behind
For she did not lose consciousness of her sins

Sinners

It is our plight

For which we cannot escape

Until our hearts turn back

To the One who gives hearts life

We were not born sinners

We are partial to be

Sinners

Beneficial actions of purifying the heart (based on the commentary of Imam Al-Mawlud's Matharat Al-Qulub translated by Sheikh Hamza Yusuf)

The heart adheres to actions that are consistent and undeviating whether or not they are small.

Good actions clandestinely fulfilled purely for the sake of God and out of wonder and love for God.

When one is free of worldly desires, his actions become of the purest.

And those endeavoured out of hope shine brighter and aristocratic.

All of these are actions benefiting for purifying the heart.

Forgiveness

Forgiveness does not mean they are off the hook. It does not mean to trust them again, or to let them back in. It does not mean that they have won. Plenty a time, we have been told that holding on to grudges, hate and resentment is like drinking poison and expecting the other person to die. Do we really understand what it means?

It is in the act of letting go of the resentment and harbouring no grudges against those responsible for the hurts and grief, that our hearts find healing. We set our hearts free from the prison of the violations which others have committed. It is in this peaceful act that our hearts find God.

Do you see?

You are a treasured gem

So precious

Your life is of value

There is a purpose to your existence

Do you see?

Is there anyone who claims to be your friend,

And then reminds you of all your imperfections?

Is there anyone who claims to care about you

Then, when you slip, they say you are worthless and hopeless

And there is nothing about you to be proud of.

Is there anyone who claims to love you

And then throws insults in your way
To degrade you.

Do you see?

Why do you remain imprisoned by the opinions of others,
When there is nothing to justify?
Why do you remain in prison,
When the door to your future is wide open?

Do you see?

Why do you search in others,
For that which you can find only within yourself and the Creator?
You are a precious gem
If only you knew.

Don't despair in that which is non-existent.

Part your ways

Awaken your true potential

Spread your wings

And fly.

Do you see???

Amina G

You should know, my dear friend.

Once upon a time
In this journey of life
We held each other
Through dark times
We reminded each other
Of hope
Of happiness
Of love
Together, we searched for abundance
Through friendship
And sisterhood

You should know, my dear friend
It was not enough
To fix my bleeding heart
To heal my bleeding wounds

Prose of The Travelling Soul

To remove my nightmares
To escape the night terrors
To fill the void of emptiness
To veil the feeling of worthlessness

You should know, my dear friend
If I have to embark
On this journey Without you
This is where we part ways

May you be at peace with yourself.
Never despair.

You should know, my dear friend
I did not change my life to hurt you
I changed it to save me.

Amina G

If you need me to tell you...

If you need me to tell you
One could never quite fathom,
The girl that was me
Before the guidance
Perhaps if one knew
One might find
Somewhere in the heart
An ounce of appreciation

If you need me to tell you
About the lost, troubled, confused
Angry little girl
Overpowered by fear and anxiety

If you need me to tell you
About the nightmares

Night terrors
Hallucinations
Images
Faceless faces
The mind could not elucidate
Overpowered by fear and anxiety

If you need me to tell you
About the bitter draught
Broken and damaged woman

If you need me to tell you
That in the religion
There is healing
There is Mercy
There is solace
There is contentment
A joy that is felt, even when alone

There is a purpose

There is LOVE

If you need me to tell you

I did not change my life to hurt you

I changed it to save me.

My lost soul

In the grievance of my lost soul

Was the persistent search for something

Which ceased to exist

Only for a time

And the lack of understanding

Of the life that awaits.

Scrutiny of the mind

I am a mirror of everything you see.

The story you don't understand.

The loudest voice in your head.

The calmest whisper in your head.

The one you tried to break.

The one you tried to fix.

The vision.

The energy.

I am a depiction of you.

A reflection of you.

The one you see everywhere you go.

I am YOU.

Dreams

I dreamed a dream
A memory from bygone days
In Your face I saw
A Saving grace
My mind betrayed
An illusion
To decoy myself in time
A paradigm
Non-existent

Your stares
Elicited a turbulence
My head in conflict
confusion
My soul agitated.
Thirsty for answers

To questions I could not ask.
In my mind a pitiful chorus
To a blank canvas.

Slowly you faded away
Into the distance
Gone
Forever.

A change from within

Chasing
Love. Worth. Assurance.
Seeking validation
Chasing desperately,
Words you need to hear.
Until you blue
Your heart bruised
Your value graded on sentiments.
Psychological detriments.

Changed on the outside to
Change opinions.
Clinging on for their acceptance
From yourself you run.
It is time to stop running
Stop burning

Amina G

Your life
You are a blessing.

Recite and reflect on the words of your Lord.

Indeed, God will not change the condition of a people until they change what is in themselves. Qur'an 13:11

Your change will come.
What you seek is from within you.
Embrace the you within
Your only medicine.

Discipline. Sacrifices (for yourself).
Your strength from God. Faith:
Self love
Self worth
Self confidence

Hold firmly, the gravity of these qualities.

Through faith and conviction,

You will overcome

This life's cuts and bruises,

Even the wound that oozes.

Last words

Those whom I have wronged,
I ask for your forgiveness.
I seek forgiveness from God.
May God mend what I have broken.

My love to family and friends
Who have been there
Through the best of times
And the worst of times.

Those ended companies
Though our friendships gone
I'm grateful (more than words), the happy times, the hardships we got through.
I'm grateful we were once a part of each other.

Prose of The Travelling Soul

As nothing lasts forever and
Paths take different turns.
I'm grateful, I will always remember
Say a prayer for you.

Those who have helped me
I sincerely thank you
From the bottom of my heart.
May God reward you immensely.
May God give you the good of this world and the next.
May God protect you.
May you always be blessed.

Glory be to God.
There is no power or strength except from God.
God is the Greatest.
Praised is He.

Beautiful reminders for the soul

We are not our past. We are not our mistakes. Our past does not determine who we are. Our mistakes do not define us. Other people's judgements are not an interpretation of our individuality. We were by nature created with imperfections. Every day is a new day to set things right. To do better. To be better. We have God. We have His love. We are surrounded by His mercy. Nothing is greater than that.

The religion of excellence

Islam is not a religion of striving for perfection but striving for excellence. By striving for excellence, we do everything we can to the best of our ability. When we try to be perfect in the religion, it becomes a dangerous act for we then end up transmuting to the opposite of our end goal. Striving to become the "perfect" Muslim can make the heart anxious. So instead of perfection, strive for excellence and understand the difference between the two.

Give glad tidings to the strangers "Islam began as something strange, and it shall return to being something strange as it began. So, give glad tidings to the strangers."

— PROPHET MUHAMMAD (Peace be upon him), Sahih Muslim

———

He who created you from one soul Qur'an 7:189

The universe is a complete unique entity. Everything and everyone is bound together with some invisible strings. DO NOT BREAK ANYONE's HEART, DO NOT LOOK DOWN ON WEAKER THAN YOU. One's sorrow at the other side of the world can make the entire world suffer; one's happiness can make the entire world smile.

— Shams Tabrizi

Amina G

You suppose you are the trouble

But you are the cure

You suppose you are the lock on the door

But you are the key that opens it.

— RUMI

If everything seems dark,

Look again,

You may be the light.

— RUMI

Don't you know it yet,

It is your light

That lights the worlds.

— RUMI

The world needs more of

Your love

Your patience

Your kindness

More of your calm.

Remember to smile.

When you smile,

You make it easy.

Books for the soul

Qur'an, a new translation by M.A.S Abdel Haleem

Purification of the heart, a translation & commentary of Imam Al-Mawlud's Matharat Al-Qulub by Sheikh Hamza

Muhammad by Martin Lings

Vision of Islam by Sachiko Murata & William C Chittick

Inner dimensions of worship by Al-Ghazali

The beginning of Guidance by Abu Hamid Al-Ghazali translated by Mashhad Al-Allaf

Dua's for the contentment of the heart

www.mtp.agency

www.facebook.com/mtp.agency

@mtp_agency

www.ingramcontent.com/pod-product-compliance
Ingram Content Group UK Ltd.
Pitfield, Milton Keynes, MK11 3LW, UK
UKHW022209230426
12048UKWH00016BA/742